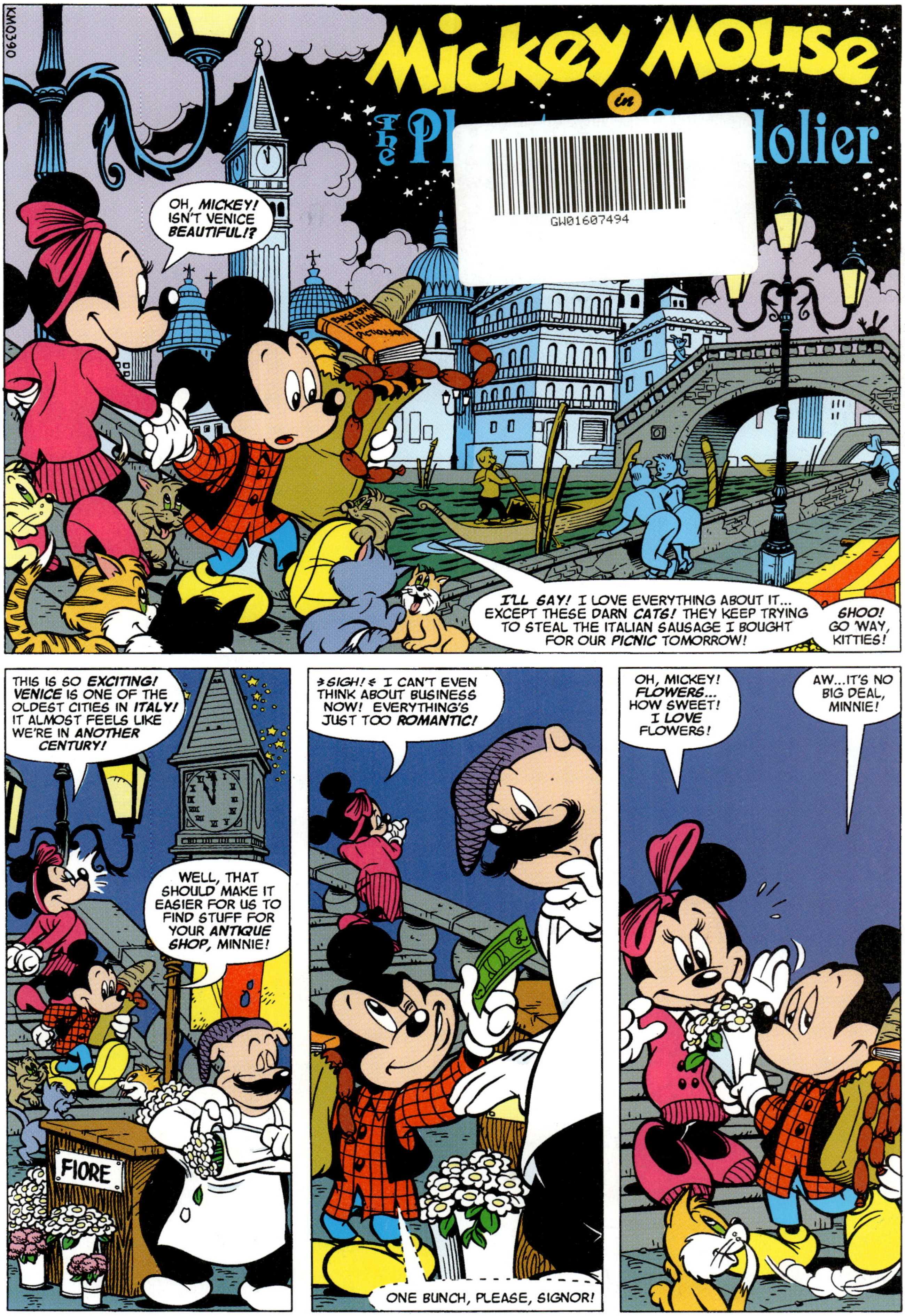

KM0390

Mickey Mouse

in

GW01607494

OH, MICKEY! ISN'T VENICE **BEAUTIFUL!?**

I'LL SAY! I LOVE EVERYTHING ABOUT IT... EXCEPT THESE DARN **CATS!** THEY KEEP TRYING TO STEAL THE ITALIAN SAUSAGE I BOUGHT FOR OUR **PICNIC** TOMORROW!

SHOO! GO 'WAY, KITTIES!

£4.95

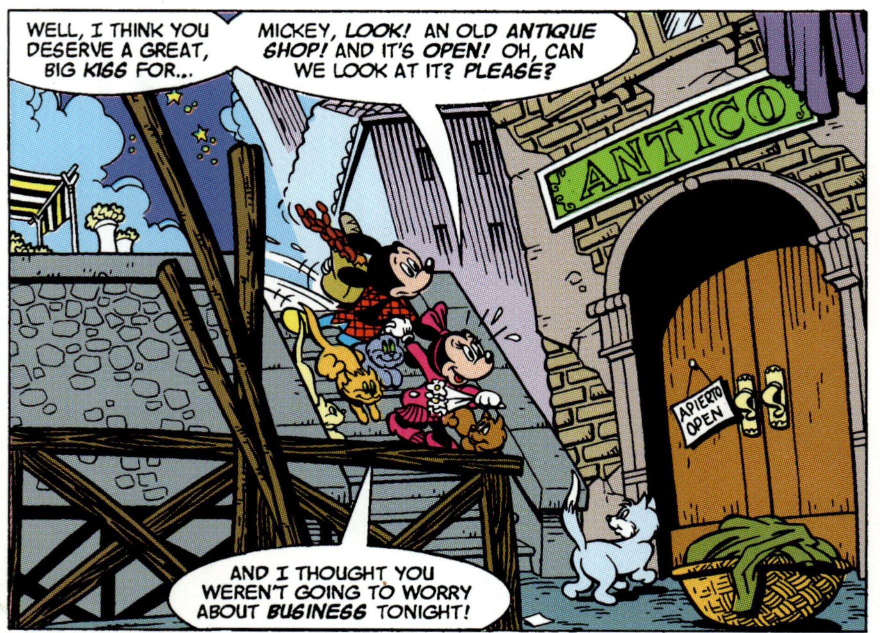
WELL, I THINK YOU DESERVE A GREAT, BIG KISS FOR...
MICKEY, LOOK! AN OLD ANTIQUE SHOP! AND IT'S OPEN! OH, CAN WE LOOK AT IT? PLEASE?
ANTICO
APIERTO OPEN
AND I THOUGHT YOU WEREN'T GOING TO WORRY ABOUT BUSINESS TONIGHT!

NO WONDER THIS PLACE IS OPEN SO LATE...IT MUST BE A TOURIST TRAP! MOST OF THESE ANTIQUES ARE JUST JUNK, IF YOU ASK M--
MICKEY, LOOK!
40 WT.

THIS NECKLACE IS BEAUTIFUL!
PERICOLO! NON TOCCARE!

MINNIE! DON'T PUT THAT ON! THAT SIGN SAYS-- DANGER! DO NOT TOUCH!
ENGLISH ITALIAN DICTIONARY
OH, NO!

THE EVIL ONE'S NECKLACE! TAKE IT OFF, QUICKLY!
OH! I...I CAN'T! IT WON'T COME OFF!

THEN IT IS ALREADY TOO LATE
YOU ARE CURSED! NOW THE PHANTOM GONDOLIER WILL GET YOU!

SIGNORA, I DON'T KNOW ANYTHING ABOUT A CURSE, BUT CAN'T YOU HELP US GET THIS NECKLACE OFF? IT'S STUCK! AND SOMETHING'S WRONG WITH MINNIE!
IT'S THE CURSE! GO BEFORE THE BOATMAN COMES!

WHO IS THIS SPOOK YOU KEEP TALKING ABOUT?
HE IS THE ONE WHO PLACED THE CURSE ON THE NECKLACE! SOON, HE WILL RETURN TO RECLAIM IT...

...AND TO CARRY AWAY THE POOR GIRL WHO WEARS IT!
ANTICO
SPLOOSH SPLOOSH

HUH? B-BUT MINNIE IS...
I KNOW! SOON YOUR MINNIE WILL BE TAKEN TO THE SHADOWLAND TO BE HIS BRIDE!

BEFORE THE TOWER CLOCK STRIKES MIDNIGHT, HE WILL COME IN HIS GHOSTLY GONDOLA TO TAKE HER AWAY! ONCE THEY DRIFT PAST THE OLD RIALTO BRIDGE...SHE WILL BE HIS FOREVER!
NOW, WAIT A MINUTE...

LOOK FOR YOURSELF IF YOU DOUBT ME! OUTSIDE!
HUH?

OHMIGOSH! MINNIE...STOP!
IT IS TOO LATE! THE BOATMAN'S MAGIC MUSIC HAS PUT HER IN A TRANCE! SHE IS HIS NOW!
ANTICO

I'VE GOT TO RUN DOWN THERE AND STOP HIM!

NO! YOU CAN'T! IT'S TOO DANGEROUS! HE IS SO EVIL THAT HIS VERY TOUCH...
...MEANS DEATH!

OHMIGOSH! HE TOUCHED THOSE FLOWERS AND THEY DIED!
OH, I WISH WE COULD HELP HER!

BUT WHAT CAN WE DO?
EVEN IF WE COULD HELP...SHE IS TOO FAR AWAY TO REACH IN TIME!
THERE MUST BE SOMETHING WE CAN...

WAIT A MINUTE!
THIS SAUSAGE I BOUGHT!

IF THOSE CATS DOWN THERE ARE STILL HUNGRY...

WE MAY BE ABLE TO AVOID A CATASTROPHE!
M-M-MEOW
MEOW
OH!

IT WORKED! THOSE CATS WOKE YOU UP JUST IN TIME, MINNIE! ARE YOU O.K.?
YES...BUT I FEEL LIKE I WAS DREAMING...
COME! FOLLOW ME!

COME BACK HERE! THE GIRL IS MINE!

RUN ALL YOU WANT... I'LL FIND YOU!
OH, MICKEY! I'M SCARED!
YOU AND ME BOTH, MINNIE! THAT GUY'S POISON!
COME--MY HOUSE IS NEAR. WE WILL HIDE!

WE'LL HIDE IN HERE, MINNIE! I'LL GUARD YOU!

WHEW! WELL, MINNIE WILL BE SAFE NOW. WE'RE TOO HIGH UP FOR THAT SPOOK TO GET HER!
MAYBE SO...BUT HE IS VERY TRICKY...SO WE MUST BE VERY CAREFUL. THE EVIL ONE HAS WAITED 400 YEARS FOR HIS BRIDE...AND HE WILL NOT GIVE UP EASILY.

STILL...IN 20 MINUTES IT WILL BE MIDNIGHT! IF HE DOES NOT HAVE HER BY THEN...HE WILL HAVE TO GO BACK TO THE LAND OF GHOSTS WITHOUT HER!
THEN WE'VE GOTTA MAKE SURE HE STAYS AWAY!
I NEED INFORMATION! CAN YOU TELL ME ANYTHING ABOUT HIM, MA'AM?
"I SHOULD START WITH THE NECKLACE..."
MY NAME IS SIGNORA ROSA DI MOUSINI...AND THE NECKLACE HAS BEEN IN MY FAMILY FOR CENTURIES... EVER SINCE THE EVIL ONE GAVE IT TO MY GREAT-GREAT-GREAT-AUNT ELIZABETA DI MOUSINI.
G-GOSH!
"EVEN THEN HE WAS A GREAT MAGICIAN... BUT VERY EVIL!
"WITH HIS MAGIC PIPES HE COULD MAKE TREES AND FLOWERS BEND AND GROW INTO MANY HORRIBLE SHAPES!
"...HE WANTED TO MARRY ELIZABETA... BUT SHE FEARED HIM. AS A TOKEN OF HIS LOVE, HE GAVE HER THE NECKLACE!
"KNOWING OF HER FEAR, ELIZABETA'S FATHER ORDERED THE EVIL ONE TO STAY AWAY FROM HIS DAUGHTER. WHEN HE REFUSED, HER FATHER, A POWERFUL NOBLEMAN, ORDERED HIM ARRESTED!"

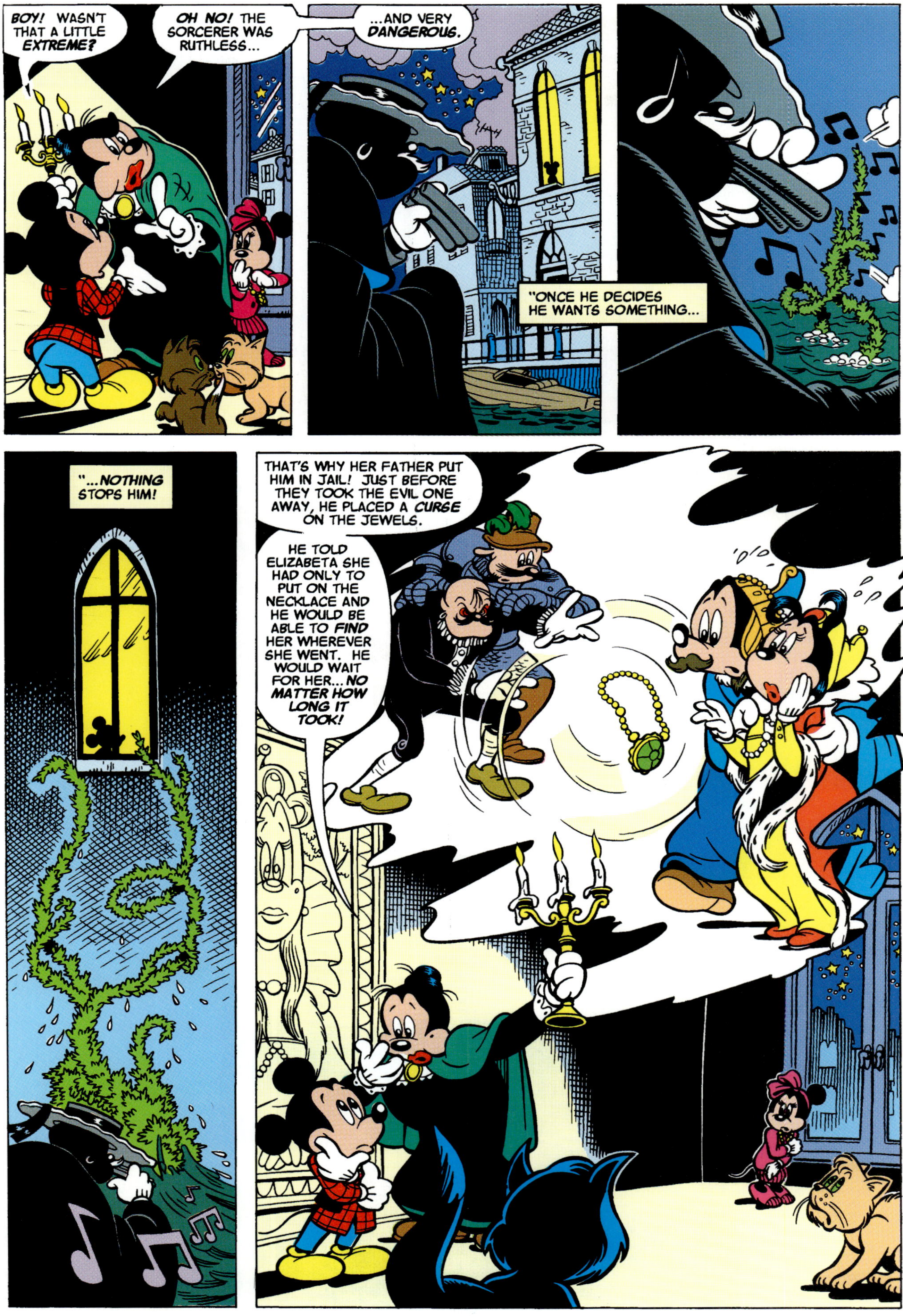

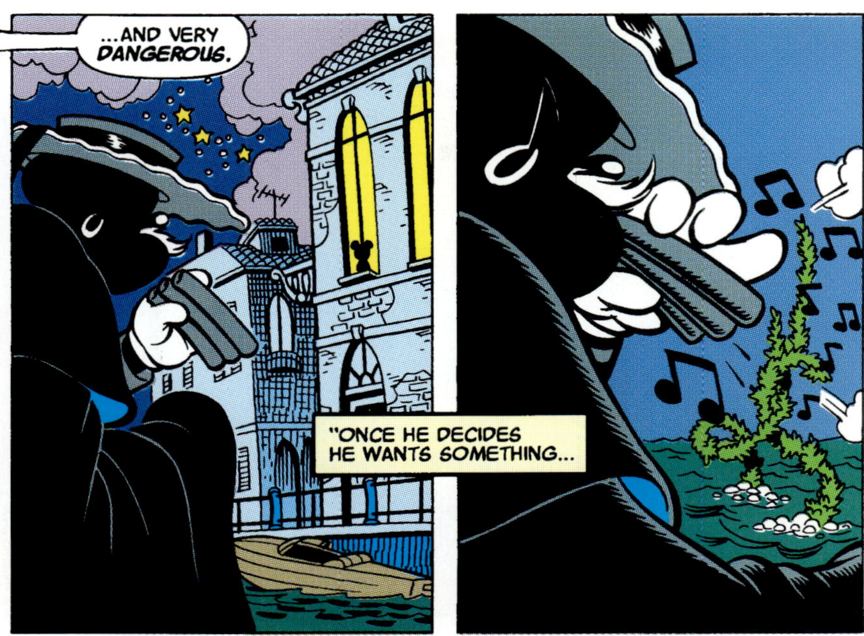

THAT'S WHY HER FATHER PUT HIM IN JAIL! JUST BEFORE THEY TOOK THE EVIL ONE AWAY, HE PLACED A CURSE ON THE JEWELS.

HE TOLD ELIZABETA SHE HAD ONLY TO PUT ON THE NECKLACE AND HE WOULD BE ABLE TO FIND HER WHEREVER SHE WENT. HE WOULD WAIT FOR HER... NO MATTER HOW LONG IT TOOK!

ELIZABETA WAS TOO AFRAID TO WEAR THE NECKLACE...AFTER SHE DIED, IT PASSED DOWN THROUGH MY FAMILY...UNTIL I FOOLISHLY PUT IT ON DISPLAY TO ATTRACT PEOPLE TO MY SHOP!
SINCE THE SORCERER DIED, HIS GHOST HAS DRIFTED DOWN THE CANALS SEARCHING FOR ELIZABETA. WHEN SIGNORINA MINNIE PUT ON HIS NECKLACE, THE GHOST THOUGHT SHE WAS ELIZABETA!
WHEW! WHAT A STORY! I--

CRASH
WHAT??

HELP!
I'LL SAVE YOU, MINNIE!
ALL IS LOST! YOU CAN DO NOTHING!

IN TWO MINUTES THEY WILL REACH THE BRIDGE. ONCE THEY PASS UNDER IT...SHE WILL BE HIS FOREVER!
NOT IF I CAN HELP IT! SIGNORA ROSA...DO YOU HAVE A BOAT?

YES...AND YOU MAY USE IT, MY LITTLE FRIEND! BUT I BEG YOU NOT TO!
HIS MAGIC IS TOO GREAT! HE WILL DESTROY YOU IF YOU TRY!
YEAH? WELL, HE'S GOT MINNIE, AND THAT MEANS THAT BAG OF BONES JUST MIGHT FIND OUT THAT MICKEY MOUSE HAS A FEW TRICKS, TOO!

NOW... COME ON, MOTOR... START!!!

AH, MY ELIZABETA! IN A MOMENT WE WILL CROSS THE THRESHOLD TO ETERNITY!

IT HAS BEEN A LONG TIME, ELIZABETA!
YOU TAKE ME BACK RIGHT NOW! AND MY NAME ISN'T ELIZABETA! IT'S MINNIE!

YOU WEAR THE NECKLACE I GAVE YOU... THEREFORE YOU ARE MY ELIZABETA ...EVEN IF YOU LOOK DIFFERENT!

AND ONCE WE PASS UNDER THIS BRIDGE...NO ONE CAN SAVE YOU!
OH, YEAH? WELL MAYBE YOU'D BETTER TELL HIM!
VRRRRROO

OH?! WHO...?

NO!
MICKEY!
GRAB MY HAND AND HOLD ON TIGHT, MINNIE!
VRROOMMM!!
SPLOOSH!

MY HERO! YOU GOT HERE JUST IN TIME! THANKS FOR SAVING ME, MICKEY!
WE'RE NOT OUT OF THE SOUP YET, MINNIE!
I JUST WANT TO GET US OUT OF HERE BEFORE HE PULLS SOME OTHER TRICK!
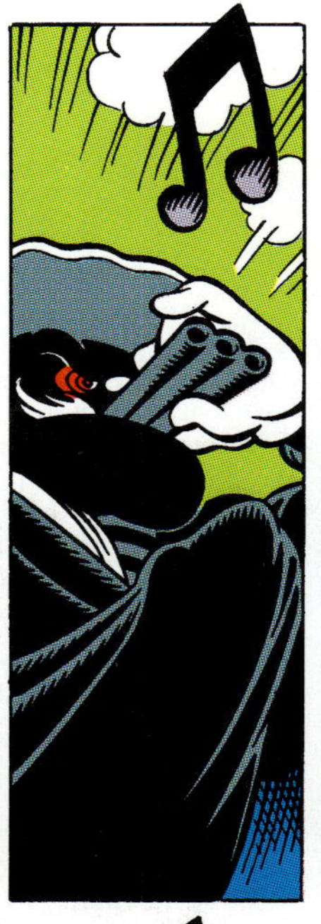

MICKEY! LOOK AT ALL THAT SEAWEED! IT JUST STARTED GROWING OUT OF THE WATER!
UH-OH! I WAS AFRAID OF SOMETHING LIKE THIS! IT'S THOSE DARN MAGIC PIPES OF HIS!
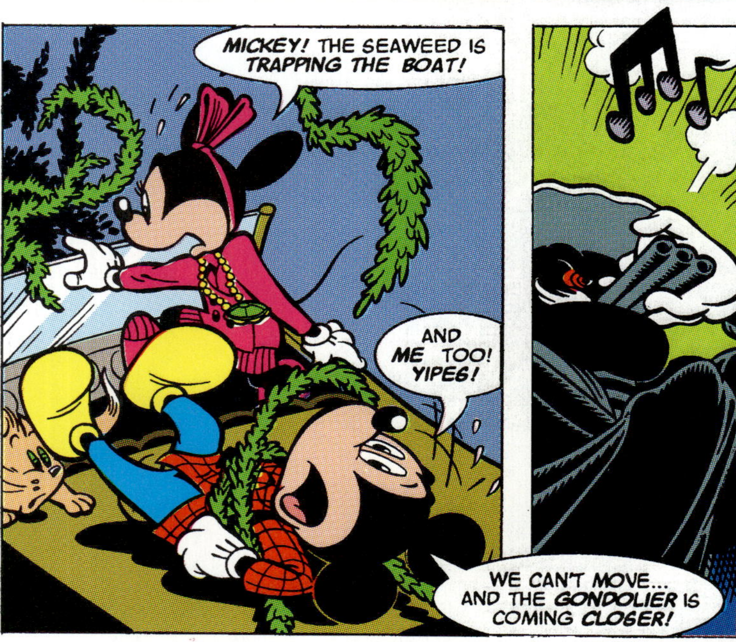
MICKEY! THE SEAWEED IS TRAPPING THE BOAT!
AND ME TOO! YIPES!
WE CAN'T MOVE... AND THE GONDOLIER IS COMING CLOSER!

GULP! IF WE CAN JUST STALL HIM A FEW MORE MINUTES, IT'LL BE MIDNIGHT...AND HE'LL HAVE TO GO BACK TO WHEREVER HE CAME FROM!
C'MON, MINNIE! I'VE GOT AN IDEA! HELP ME PULL UP THIS STRAND OF SEAWEED!
BUT, MICKEY,-- WHAT GOOD WILL THAT DO?

WE CAN'T GET THE BOAT FREE IN TIME TO ESCAPE!

I'M NOT TRYING TO FREE THE BOAT, MINNIE! I'M TRYING TO... MMPHH! ...TIE THIS PIECE OF SEAWEED...

...INTO A LASSO!
WWHOOOSH
?!
CHUNK!

IT WORKED! THE MUSIC STOPPED, AND THE SEAWEED IS LETTING GO!
YOU LITTLE PEST! YOU'LL BE SORRY YOU CROSSED ME!
BUT NOT SOON ENOUGH! HE'S ALREADY HERE!

NOW I'VE GOT YOU!
MICKEY! HE'S ON OUR BOAT!

GULP! ONE MINUTE LEFT!
HEY, YOU... CATCH!
MY MAGIC PIPES!

THEY'RE GONE!
AND MY MAGIC'S GONE, TOO!
SPLASH!

WHY, YOU LITTLE... NO! IT CAN'T BE MIDNIGHT SO SOON! IT CAN'T BE TIME FOR ME TO...

BONG! BONG!
...DISAPPEAR!

BONG! BONG! BONG!
WHEW! HE'S GONE! AND THIS TIME, HE WON'T BE BACK!
MICKEY, LOOK!

THE NECKLACE... IT CAME OFF!
WOW! THAT PROVES THE CURSE IS BROKEN!
OH, MICKEY! HOW WONDERFUL!

JUST TO PLAY IT SAFE, I'M GOING TO GET RID OF THIS THING! I KNOW SIGNORA ROSA WON'T MIND.
WHEN WE GET BACK, I'M GOING TO BUY HER A PRESENT TO REPLACE IT. WHAT SHOULD WE GET HER, MINNIE?
SPLASH

ANYTHING BUT FLOWERS, MICKEY! FOR SOME REASON...I'M SURE SHE'S SICK OF PLANTS!
HA! HA! HA!
The End

SORRY TO *COIN* A PHRASE, BUT THIS IS ONE QUIZ YOU CAN *BANK* ON. SEE HOW YOU SCORE:

LESS THAN 3 - Your piggy bank must be hungry.
3 TO 7 - The interest rate on your account is rising!
OVER 7 - You put Scrooge to shame!

1. How much do you think the earliest jeans were sold for per dozen?

- A. 50p
- B. £7
- C. £27
- D. £200

2. What relation to the nephews is Uncle Scrooge?

- A. Great Uncle
- B. Brother
- C. Long lost Uncle
- D. No relation

3. How many pennies did the Royal Mint produce in 1933?

- A. Nobody knows
- B. 1,000
- C. 4
- D. 3,000

4. Which baddies is Scrooge always protecting his money from?

- A. Bugle Boys
- B. Bad Bunch
- C. Beagle Boys
- D. Bachelor Boys

5. Where does the dollar sign originate from?

- A. The number 8, for 'pieces of 8'
- B. The number 8, for 'cat o' 9 tails'
- C. The number 8 for 10-2
- D. The letter 8 for 6+2

6. The US Mint once made a mistake on their coins. How did it read?

- A. In grotto we must
- B. In God we must
- C. In God we trussed
- D. In gold we trust

7. In 1978, if you piled up all the £1 notes in circulation, how high would the pile be?

- A. About 10km
- B. About 500km
- C. About 744km
- D. About 2,087km

8. In 1820 a man sold his wife at Canterbury Cattle Market, for how much?

- A. 1p
- B. 5 shillings (25p)
- C. £1,000
- D. £20

9. What is Scrooge's lucky charm?

- A. A gold locket
- B. A fish which he keeps in a jar
- C. A lucky dime he keeps in a glass case
- D. A cuddly, soft toy

ANSWERS: 1.(B) 2.(A) 3.(C) 4.(C) 5.(A) 6.(D)
7.(C) 8.(B) 9.(C)

MAGIC PENNY

"I can make money appear," I told Scrooge, one day. "It's an easy and fool-proof way to get rich quick!"

CLUE: The trick is not to let your audience see the paper attached to the bottom of the cup!

Here's how it's done:

1. Cut off the bottom of a paper cup.
2. Draw a circle around the rim on a piece of paper, then cut out the circle.
3. Glue the circle you have cut out on to the rim of the cup. Now use a sheet of the same paper and place the penny on top, when no one is looking.
4. Then, with the cup in place, ask your friends to look down through the top of the cup. They can't see the penny. Pull the cup away and 'hey presto', the penny appears. Magic!

UNCLE $CROOGE
in
A CHEAP MEAL
D-4245/
KU4390
GOOD GRIEF! PRICES CERTAINLY HAVE GONE UP SINCE THE LAST TIME I BOUGHT MY OWN DINNER!

THEN AGAIN, THAT WAS FIFTEEN YEARS AGO, HEH, HEH!

SIGH! NOW THAT I KNOW WHAT I WANT, THE WAITER HAS DISAPPEARED!

OH, WELL! I'LL JUST NIBBLE ON THIS BREAD!

HEY! THIS STUFF IS PRETTY GOOD! AT LEAST I WON'T STARVE 'TIL THE WAITER SHOWS UP!

MUNCH! MUNCH! THIS BREAD IS QUITE DELICIOUS, AS A MATTER OF FACT!

URP! NEVER MIND, WAITER! I'M TOO FULL TO ORDER DINNER NOW! AND THE PRICE WAS RIGHT, TOO! JUST LIKE THE GOOD OLD DAYS!
End

Pluto™

EVERY BANK HOLIDAY ... THAT BIG TURKEY DINNER MEANS THE **SAME THING** TO PLUTO! BONES... **BONES**... **BONES... BUT...**

NO, PLUTO! NO TURKEY BONES FOR YOU! YOU KNOW THEY AREN'T GOOD FOR DOGS! THEY SPLINTER!

KG-0390

AND THIS YEAR... IT LOOKS LIKE THE SAME ROUTINE IS STARTING **ALL OVER AGAIN!**

WHY CAN'T BANK HOLIDAYS BE **STEAK** EATING DAYS (THINKS PLUTO)! **STEAKS** HAVE **REAL KEEN BONES!**

BUT SAY... WHAT'S THIS? OH, HO! IF THAT SILLY GOBBLER HAPPENED TO GET AWAY...

...THE MENU MIGHT **HAVE** TO BE STEAK... AND **THEN** THERE'D BE GOOD **EATIN' BONES!**

AND SO...'TWAS THE NIGHT BEFORE THE HOLIDAY AND ALL THROUGH THE HOUSE, NOT A CREATURE WAS STIRRING...
Z Z
Z Z Z
...NOT EVEN MICKEY MOUSE!
BUT...'TWAS A DIFFERENT STORY OUT IN THE YARD! PLUTO WAS CHEWING FAST AND HARD!
GAWK!
CHOMP! CHOMP!

HMM ... A PHONE CALL...

AWAY WITH THAT SILLY BANK HOLIDAY LUNCH, AND BACK TO THE BONES THAT YOU CAN MUNCH!
GOBBLE! GOBBLE!
R-R-RING

YAWN...HELLO! OH, HORACE HORSECOLLAR, CALLING LONG DISTANCE? SURE ...PUT HIM ON!

YES, HORACE! OF COURSE YOUR TURKEY'S SAFE! IT'S RIGHT IN MY BACK YARD NOW! ENJOY YOUR VISIT BACK IN THE OLD HOME TOWN! I'LL TAKE GOOD CARE OF IT!

WHAT'S THAT? ME? EAT YOUR TURKEY? DON'T WORRY! WE'RE HAVING STEAK AT OUR HOUSE!

YES, THAT'S RIGHT! STEAK! THIS YEAR I DECIDED TO BE DIFFERENT!
!

THE TRUTH STRIKES PLUTO LIKE A SLEDGE HAMMER!
BONK!

THE TURKEY HE HAD RELEASED... DIDN'T EVEN BELONG TO MICKEY!
GOOD-BYE, HORACE!
CLICK!

MICKEY'D BEEN PLANNING A STEAK DINNER ALL ALONG!
HORACE SURE THINKS A LOT OF THAT TURKEY!
GULP

IF ANYTHING **HAPPENS** TO THAT PRIZE GOBBLER, **HORACE WILL NEVER FORGIVE MICKEY!**

AND **MICKEY** WILL NEVER FORGIVE . . .

PLUTO JUST **HAS** TO CATCH THAT TURKEY!

BUT UNFORTUNATELY... HE ISN'T THE **ONLY ONE** WITH THAT IDEA!

THE CHASE GETS HOTTER...AND ROUGHER!

WELL, WHAT DO YOU KNOW! GAWRSH! MICKEY'LL SURE BE GLAD TO HEAR ABOUT THIS!

MEANWHILE... THE CHASE HAS LED TO **THE MERRYLAND FUN PARK!**

OOPS! WHERE DID ALL THESE RELATIVES COME FROM? (THINKS PLUTO)!

OKAY! IF THAT'S THE WAY THEY WANT IT, US DOGS WILL SHOW 'EM A THING OR TWO!

BONK!
?

HM-M-M... SO THAT'S IT! IT'S ALL DONE WITH MIRRORS!

CRUNCH!
YEOW

SEEMS LIKE A DOG CAN'T EVEN TRUST A **REFLECTION** THESE DAYS!
HEY! YOU HEARD ME! YOU CAN'T PLAY YOUR TURKEY TIG GAMES IN **HERE**!

NOW STAY **OUT**!

WELL... THIS IS **ONE** WAY TO CATCH UP WITH THIS GOOFY GOBBLER!

OOF!
AWK!

BUT **STAYING** WITH HIM IS A TOUGHER PROBLEM!
LOOK, OSCAR! A DOG RIDING A TURKEY!
OR IS IT A TURKEY RIDING A DOG?

WHICHEVER IT IS... IT'S IMPOSSIBLE! PLUTO WILL NEVER BE ABLE TO...
WHIRL A WAY

BUT WAIT A MINUTE! HE CAN STILL TRY STRATEGY! AND BY GOLLY... HE WILL!
HERE WE GO!

THIS BRINGS TURKEY TO THAT LOVELY **DONE-IN** COMPLEXION YOU'RE SURE TO LIKE...

BROKE LOOSE? OH, WELL...(THINKS PLUTO) IF MICKEY WANTS TO FEEL **THAT** WAY ABOUT IT...THAT'S OKAY!

PUZZLER PAGE
FLOWER POWER
P L F F A D Y P K
V I O L E T S Z P
O L O S O V N W A
X Y F M K O A U B
P P E E V O P S D
B A S D F X L H P
E B O V S U A L F
C A R N A T I O N
S V O R C H I D W
There are six common flower names buried in this word search puzzle. See if you can spot them!
OVER THE MOON
S O O N J S E
P W N O U P P
G L I O N R R
F T U N E X U
B A L L O O N
S K P V I F E
ALL WRAPPED UP!
Wow! That's a nice present, Louie! Unscramble the letters and you'll be able to tell him what's inside.
Clue: Louie's present only has 8 letters in it!
Webbigail has gone all moon-struck! She has buried six words in this puzzle that rhyme with moon. Spoon them out for her!
ANSWERS:
FLOWER POWER: VIOLET, ROSE, CARNATION, ORCHID, PANSY, LILY. OVER THE MOON: SOON, TUNE, BALLOON, JUNE, NOON, PRUNE. ALL WRAPPED UP: COMPUTER.

DONALD DUCK
The Traveling Trio

SCRAM, URCHINS! GO PLAY OUTSIDE! I'VE GOT TO CLEAN THE HOUSE BEFORE DAISY ARRIVES!
D-2312

AND YOU KNOW HOW FUSSY SHE IS ABOUT A CLEAN HOUSE! SO I WANT YOU ALL TO STAY OUTSIDE SO YOU CAN'T MAKE A MESS OF THE HOUSE!

IT'S TAKEN ME ALL DAY TO GET THIS PLACE SPOTLESS, EVEN DAISY WON'T BE ABLE TO COMPLAIN!

GOOD GRIEF! A SPECK OF DUST! HOW ON EARTH DID I MISS THAT?

NOW I THINK I'LL MAKE A BIG JUG OF LEMONADE! IT'S ALWAYS BEEN HER FAVOURITE THIRST-QUENCHER!

EVERY TIME DAISY VISITS, UNCA DONALD HAS AN ATTACK OF CLEANING MANIA!
AT LEAST WE GET TO PLAY OUTDOORS!
WE CAN DO FUN STUFF LIKE PLAY FOOTBALL!

WATCH ME KICK IT TO THE MOON!
HEY, NOT SO HARD!
BONK!

GREAT SHOT, HUEY! YOU HIT THE CHIMNEY!
THUNK!

PLUMP!
OH, NO! IT WENT DOWN THE CHIMNEY!
UH-OH! WE'D BETTER GET IT BACK!
C'MON, GUYS! LET'S DO IT!

HOLD UP, FELLAS! I DON'T THINK YOU'RE GONNA LIKE THIS!
WHAT'S THE PROBLEM?

GASP!
BONK!
BOUNCE!

CRASH!
BUMP!
CLONK!

UNCA DONALD WILL GO RIGHT THROUGH THE ROOF WHEN HE SEES THAT MESS!
GULP! WHAT CAN WE DO?
LET'S SCRAM!

TWO MINUTES LATER...
HELLO, BOYS! WHAT'S THE HURRY?
WE'VE DECIDED TO JOIN A FOOTBALL TEAM IN TIMBUKTU!
The END

1. Here's a game that's easy to make and lots of fun. Start by sticking an empty cotton reel to a piece of strong cardboard or hardboard. The cotton reel should be towards one end of the board.

2. Push a stick, about 20 centimetres long, through the cotton reel. Then take a piece of string, about 30 centimetres long, and pin it to the top of the stick. Make a small hole in the block of wood, or a small ball, and thread the other end of the string through it.

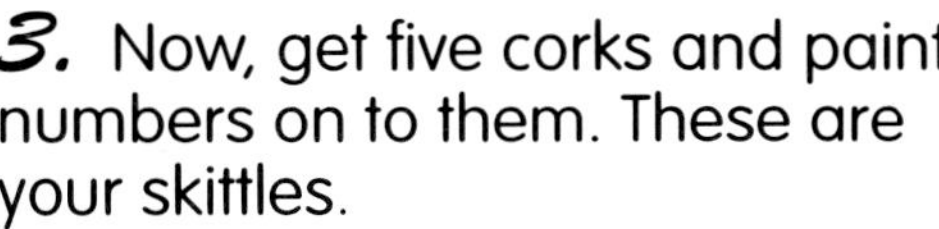

3. Now, get five corks and paint numbers on to them. These are your skittles.

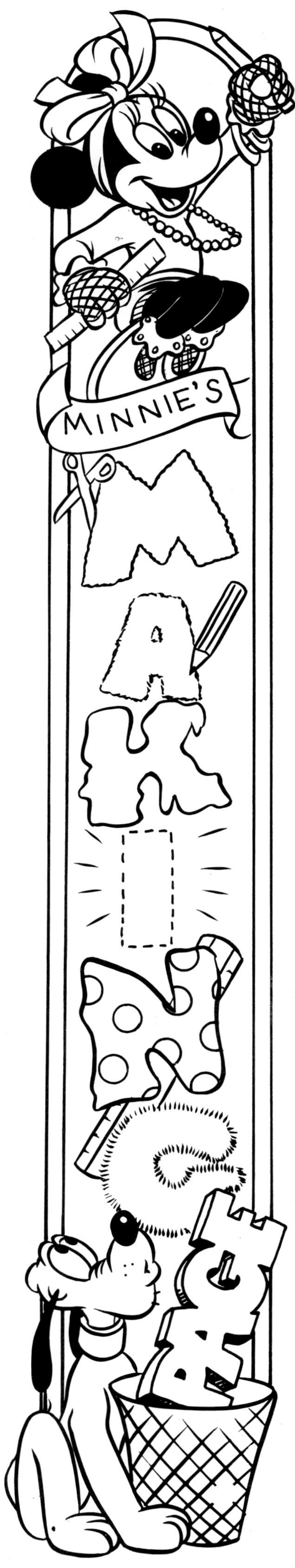

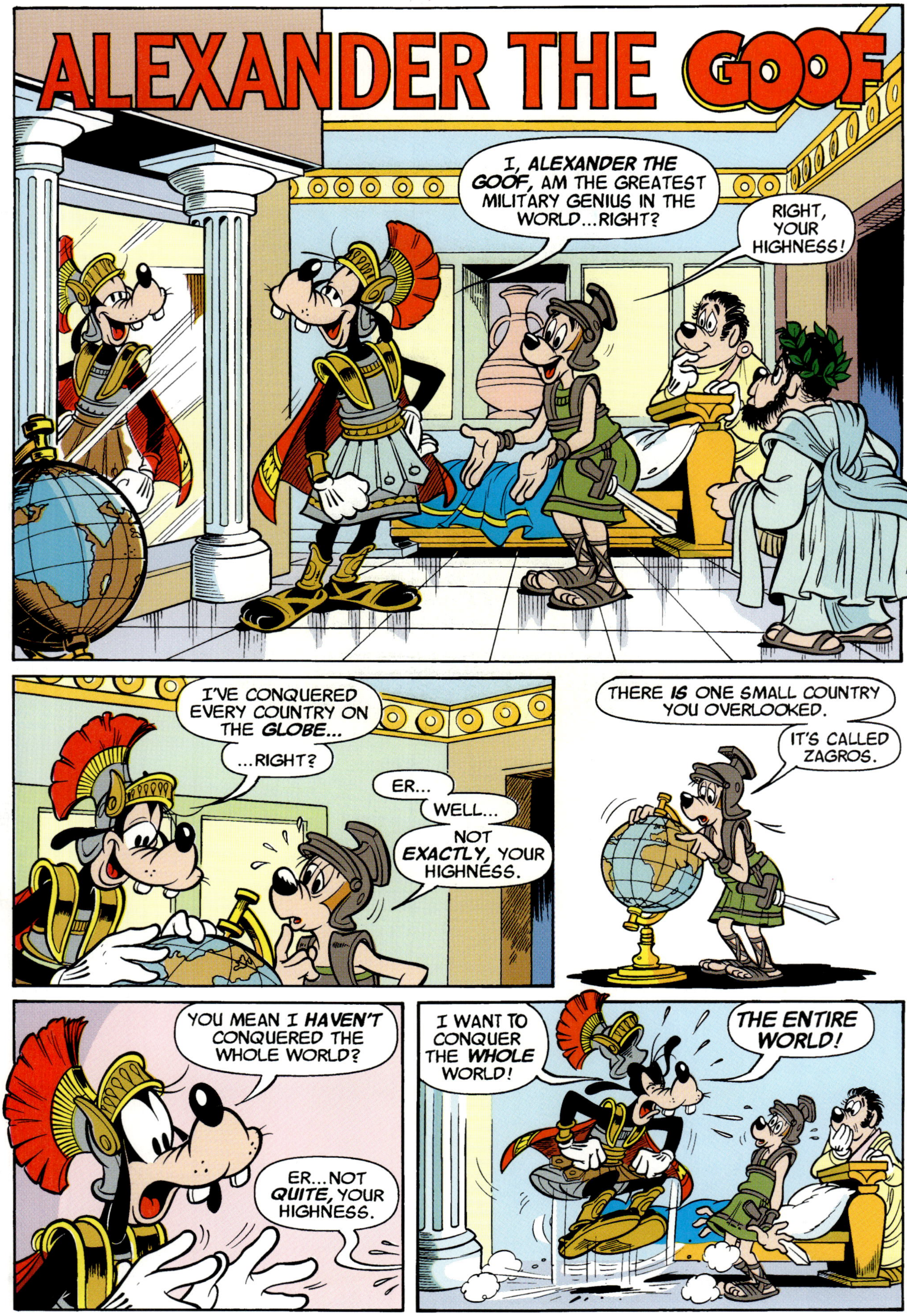

ALEXANDER THE GOOF

I, ALEXANDER THE GOOF, AM THE GREATEST MILITARY GENIUS IN THE WORLD...RIGHT?
RIGHT, YOUR HIGHNESS!

DOES THIS COUNTRY ZAGROS HAVE A LARGE ARMY?
IT HAS NO ARMY AT ALL.
GOOD! I'LL CONQUER IT IN NO TIME!
BUT IT IS PROTECTED BY THE HUGE DESERT THAT SURROUNDS IT!

WELL, NO DESERT IS GOING TO STOP ALEXANDER THE GOOF!

BUT IT IS ALSO SAID A FIRE-BREATHING DRAGON PROTECTS THE COUNTRY FROM INVADERS!

NO PROBLEM! WE'LL BRING LOTS OF WATER!
WE MARCH AT DAWN! PREPARE THE PROVISIONS... AND DON'T FORGET THE BEACH TOWELS, SUN OIL AND MARSHMALLOWS.
YES, YOUR HIGHNESS.

DAYS LATER...
NOTHING BUT DESERT AND MORE DESERT.
THE MEN CAN'T TAKE MUCH MORE OF THIS HEAT.
WAIT...I THINK I SEE SOMETHING UP AHEAD.

MAYBE IT'S JUST A MIRAGE.
IF ONLY IT WAS... BUT I THINK IT'S THE DRAGON THAT GUARDS THE COUNTRY.

GULP! WE DON'T STAND A CHANCE!
PULL YOURSELF TOGETHER, MAN!

HE'S CHARGING!
OKAY, NOW YOU CAN FALL APART!

BRING THE WATER CANNON INTO POSITION!

RUMBLE RUMBLE RUMBLE

STOMP!
STOMP!
STOMP!

START PUMPING!

PUMPA-PUMPA-
PUMPA-PUMPA-
PUMPA-PUMPA-
PUMPA-PUMP

Drip!

HOW'S THAT WATER COMING?
ROAR!
YOW!

HOW'S THAT WATER COMING?

RUN!
HELP!

GULP!

HEY! WAIT FOR ME!

MEN! WHAT HAPPENED TO THE WATER?
WE DRANK IT!
YOU SAID WE COULD!
YEAH! IT WAS HOT!

BUT I SAID ONLY ONE DRINK!

WE ONLY HAD ONE DRINK!
YEAH! ALL 20,000 OF US!

LATER...AT A STAFF MEETING...
GENTLEMEN, IT'S TIME TO CONSIDER OUR OPTIONS!
RUNNING?
FLEEING!
SWIMMING'S OUT!

ANY CHANCE OF RAIN?
NOPE!
HOW ABOUT THE INDIAN RAINMAKER?
HE'S ON HOLIDAY THIS WEEK!

THE NEAREST OASIS IS 300 MILES!
THE WATER GUY DOESN'T DELIVER UNTIL FRIDAY!
THE FIRE SERVICES ARE FOR EMERGENCIES ONLY!

GENTLEMEN, I'VE CONSIDERED OUR OPTIONS, AND I'VE REACHED A CONCLUSION!

WE'RE DOOMED!

ALEXANDER, YOU MUST SAVE US!
YEAH! YOU CAN DO IT!

YOU'RE RIGHT! I CAN DO IT!

...I THINK.

AND THINK ALEXANDER DID.
GAWRSH! WHAT'LL I DO?

AT DAWN, ALEXANDER THE GOOF MARCHED TO FACE HIS DESTINY.
I HATE TO FACE DRAGONS FIRST THING IN THE MORNING!

SNORT! YOU AGAIN!

NOW I'M *REALLY* GONNA FRY YOUR BISCUITS!
GOOD!

HUH?
BUT I'D RATHER YOU TOAST MY *MARSHMALLOWS*.

MEAN, NASTY, FIRE-BREATHING DRAGONS DON'T TOAST MARSHMALLOWS!
THEN WHAT GOOD ARE YA?
I HATE TO PULL RANK... BUT AS CONQUERER OF THE WORLD, I INSIST YOU TOAST THESE MARSHMALLOWS.

YOU INSIST?
I INSIST.
OH, YEAH?
YEAH.
WELL, LISTEN, BUDDY...
I'M LISTENING, FURNACE BREATH!

GET YOURSELF A BARBECUE! I'M LEAVING!

HOORAY! THE DRAGON'S GONE!
THREE CHEERS FOR ALEXANDER THE GOOF!
YEAH!

...AND THAT DAY ALEXANDER THE GOOF MARCHED INTO THE CITY. HE HAD LEARNED A VALUABLE LESSON... YOU DON'T HAVE TO BE A MARSHMALLOW TO TOAST MARSHMALLOWS
End

IMPOSSIBLE TEAR

Here's a trick to challenge your friends with. Tear a piece of paper into three sections, taking care not to tear all the way down. Then give the paper to a friend and ask him or her to hold each end, as Donald is doing (left), and tear it into three pieces. It can't be done, of course. One piece will always tear off in one hand.

Then show your friend how to do it. Grip the middle of the paper in your mouth and then pull each end. No problem!

COUNT THE COINS

Can you solve this little problem? Take six coins and place them in an 'L' shape. Then, by moving one coin, see if you can arrange them in an 'L' shape with four coins in each bar.

The answer is easy! Just take the end coin and place it over the coin in the corner!

BE SEATED

Here's a really crafty trick. Tell someone that you can sit somewhere that they cannot. They won't believe you. Then sit on a chair and immediately get up. No doubt they will sit exactly where you sat. Now sit on their lap. They can't sit on their own lap, can they?

TRIANGULAR TALES

Ancient .... began building pyramids for their dead Pharoahs, (kings) nearly .... y ago. The three biggest pyramids can be found at ...., near Cairo.

The dead Pharoah was placed with all his treasures in a room inside the pyramid. But wi a few years .... usually found a way in and stole any valuables.

No one can be sure how the great pyramids were built. They may have been built by ...... labour, or by Egyptian volunteers.

The stones were hauled down the ....river from ...., hundreds of miles away! The building work on each pyramid probably lasted over half a lifetime. The massive pyramic Khufu was originally 480 feet high and was built with .... blocks!

The best known Pharoah, ..., did not have a pyramid. He lived in the time when Pharoahs were buried in underground vaults. His tomb was uncovered in ...., comple with 5,000 precious objects, including sandals, beds and coffins within coffins.

THIS WAY UP...

Romans Nile 200 1937 Timbuktu
slave robbers 2,000 Kings borrowed Egyptians 5,000
Thames 10,000 Tut Aswan Cleopatra Tutankamun Giza
1922 2.3 million 1863 Bristol cows hard

Answers: Egyptians, 2,000, Giza, robbers, slave, Nile, Aswan, 2.3 million, Tutankamun, 1922

MICKEY MOUSE
in
LUNCH BREAK
KM4590/D-6850
HI, GOOFY! HOW'S YOUR NEW SANDWICH SHOP DOING?
GOOFY'S Sandwich Shop
IT'S DOING JUST GREAT, MICKEY!

HOW COME YOU'RE SHUTTING IT UP? ISN'T THE LUNCH RUSH ABOUT TO BEGIN?
SURE IS, MICK! THUH BUSIEST TIME OF THUH DAY, TOO!

SOME DAYS I'VE GOTTO MAKE ALMOST TWO HUNDRED SANDWICHES, AND--

--OMIGAWRSH! IF I DON'T HURRY UP, I'LL NEVER GET BACK HERE IN TIME! 'BYE, MICK!

GOOFY'S Sandwich Shop
GOLLY! I WONDER WHAT HE'S IN SUCH A RUSH ABOUT?

Shop
HUH--? OH, GOOFY--!
OUT TO LUNCH
End

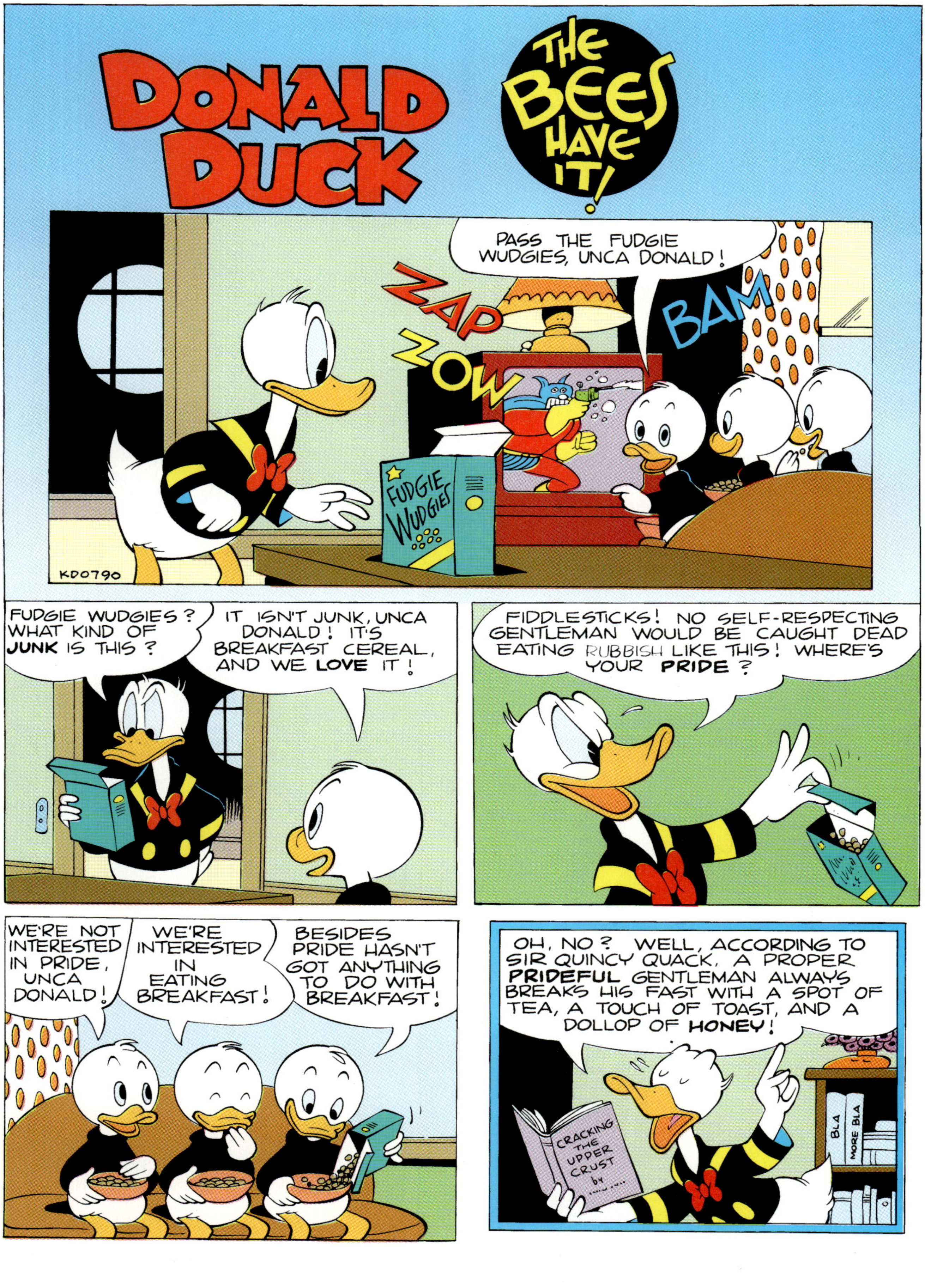

DONALD DUCK

THE BEES HAVE IT!

PASS THE FUDGIE WUDGIES, UNCA DONALD!

ZAP

ZOW

BAM

FUDGIE WUDGIES

KD0790

VERY SOON THEREAFTER~

BUT ALAS...

SORRY, SIR! THE BEES IN DUCKBURG ARE ON STRIKE! YOU WON'T FIND A JAR OF HONEY THIS SIDE OF THE MOON!
MUCH £
YES, WE DON'T ACCEPT CREDIT!
WOW

OH, YEAH? WELL THERE'S MORE THAN ONE WAY TO PEEL AN ONION!

AND UNLESS I MISS MY GUESS, I KNOW JUST WHICH WAY THAT IS!
DONALD DUCK

WHAT ON EARTH ARE YOU DOING, UNCA DONALD?
WHY ALL THE RACKET?
THE WOODS ARE FULL OF HONEY-BEES! NON-UNION ONES, TOO!

SO?
SO I'M GOING INTO THE WOODS AND LOAD UP ON ALL OF THE HONEY I WANT! AND FOR FREE!

WOULDN'T IT BE EASIER TO JUST SETTLE FOR A GENTLEMANLY BOWL OF FUDGIE WUDGIES?
ABSOLUTELY NOT! I'M GOING TO BREAK MY FAST WITH A DOLLUP OF HONEY OR KNOW THE REASON WHY!

DO YOU WANT US TO COME ALONG?
OR SHOULD WE ALERT THE HOSPITAL?

DON'T BE FUNNY! YOU STAY HERE AND KEEP THE TEA HOT! I'LL BE BACK WITH THE BEE JAM BEFORE YOU CAN SAY AFGHANISTAN BACKWARDS!

LATER

DARN! NOT A BEE IN SIGHT!

YOU'D THINK THAT ON A BEAUTIFUL SUNNY MORNING LIKE THIS THE WOODS WOULD BE BUSTLING WITH...

ZOW

A **BEE**! AND IT'S HEADED STRAIGHT FOR THAT OLD STUMP!

HOT DOG! THAT DOLLOP OF HONEY IS PRACTICALLY IN THE BAG! GENTLEMANSHIP - HERE I COME!

WAIT A MINUTE! IF I GO CHARGING INTO THAT STUMP LIKE THE CAVALRY, THOSE BEES WILL MAKE **HAMBURGER** OUT OF ME!

I'LL JUST USE A FEW OF MY GENTLEMANLY BRAINS AND CASE THE JOINT FIRST!
ONE CAN'T BE TOO CAREFUL AROUND BEES!

HMM! MIGHTY QUIET IN THERE! DO BEES TAKE COFFEE BREAKS?

EITHER THAT, OR THEY'VE ALL GONE OUT TO -

BZZT

UH-OH! IS THIS GUY A LONER, OR IS HE RIDING AROUND FOR SOMETHING WORSE?

ZAZZ
THUS

OW
HOLD STILL, UNCA DONALD! THERE'S STILL SIX DOZEN STINGERS TO GO!

BE REASONABLE, UNCA DONALD! IT'S NOT TOO LATE TO HAVE A NICE HEAPING BOWL OF –
NO! I'M GONNA BE A GENTLEMAN THIS MORNING IF IT **KILLS** ME!

WHERE'S THAT OLD **BEE** COSTUME?

YOU MEAN THE ONE THAT UNCA SCROOGE USED WHEN HE CORNERED THE HONEY MARKET IN YORBA LINDA?
YES!

IT'S HERE IN THE CLOSET, UNCA DONALD, BUT –

NO BUTS!

WITH THIS GEAR, I'LL BE IN AND OUT OF THAT OLD STUMP BEFORE THOSE SABER-TAILED KAMIKAZES KNOW I'M AROUND!
!!!
ARE YOU GUYS THINKING WHAT **I'M** THINKING?
YEP!
WE BETTER GET OUT THE FIRST AID KIT AND AN **EXTRA** PAIR OF PLIERS!

DONALD MAKES HIS WAY TOWARD THE WOODS IN AS BEE-LIKE A MANNER AS POSSIBLE!

AND HIS PROGRESS IS NOTHING IF NOT TURBULENT!

TOO ROARING, AS IT TURNS OUT!

AND SO, WHILE DONALD ENTERS THE WOODS FROM EAST . . .

. . . TWO OTHER GENTLEMAN ENTER FROM THE WEST!

A BLOAT BOTTOM IF EVER I SAW ONE, SIR!
EXACTLY!

WELL, DON'T JUST STAND THERE ADMIRING THE VIEW, GRIDLEY! GIVE THAT HONEY-HOARDING JUGGERNAUT THE WORKS! PRONTO!
YES, SIR! PRONTO! COMING RIGHT UP, SIR!
BC

BOOM

OOF! I CAN SEE NOW WHY BEES HAVE SUCH SMALL FEET!
THUD
TRIP!

GLOOP

WHAT THE DING DONG?
HEY! IT'S HONEY! PURE GRADE A, MADE IN THE WOODS, BEE JAM, AND IT'S ALL MINE!

ER-WELL, MAYBE SOME OF IT IS! HEH! HEH! HI, BOYS! HOW'RE TRICKS DOWN AT THE WAXWORKS?
NOT GOOD, EH?

HEY, WHOA! BACK OFF! AND GO EASY ON THE POLLEN, YOU DUST-RIDDEN DRONES! I'M ALLERGIC TO . . .
. . . TO . . .

ACHOO

BAZAZZZZ
SO MUCH FOR DISGUISES! I GUESS BEES DON'T SNEEZE!

YEEK! SCREECH! HELP!
VOOM

HE'S GOING CRAZY! GET A GOOD AIM AT HIM, GRIDLEY! FOR THE LOVE OF DUCKBURG, STOP HIM!
I'M TRYING, SIR! BUT HE'S MOVING BACK AND FORTH TOO FAST!

THIS IS NO TIME FOR LECTURES ON THE NICETIES OF MARKSMANSHIP, GRIDLEY! FIRE ANYWAY!
YES, SIR!

BOOM

QUACKAROONIE! NOW THOSE BUZZING NECTAR NAGGERS ARE ATTACKING IN **CLUMPS**!
ZIZZ

THWUNK

MORE BEES, YOUR SIRSHIP! TWO O'CLOCK LOW!
ZAZZ

FORGET THOSE SMALL-TIMERS! THAT BLASTED BLOAT BOTTOM IS CHARGING **US**! FIRE AGAIN!
Y-YES, SIR!
BC

SPUT
THUD

OH, WHY CAN'T THE CITY AFFORD **DECENT** CANNONS? **RETREAT**, GRIDLEY! CUT FOR THE TRUCK, AND DON'T SPARE YOUR TOOTSIES!

NO, SIR!

AND SO, ANOTHER MORNING DAWNS, AND WITH IT, ANOTHER GENTLEMANLY BREAKFAST!

YUM! YUM! This is certainly a treat not to be missed! See how you score:
LESS THAN 3 - There's a rumble in your tum!
3 TO 7 - You're prone to snack attacks!
OVER 7 - You're a gastronomic genius!

1. In 1892 a chemist called Doctor Pemberton invented which pop drink?

- A. Tizer
- B. Orangeade
- C. Coca Cola
- D. Pepsi

2. What kind of ice cream is pistachio?

- A. Mint flavoured
- B. Nut flavoured
- C. Strawberry flavoured
- D. Vanilla flavoured

3. Which gas makes fizzy drinks fizz?

- A. Sodium
- B. Moon gas
- C. Hydrogen
- D. Carbon Dioxide

4. Where was the frankfurter sausage invented?

- A. China
- B. Austria
- C. America
- D. Germany

5. What did the French call tomatoes?

- A. Love plumes
- B. Love hearts
- C. Love plums
- D. Love apples

6. Where did potato 'chips' originate?

- A. Mexico
- B. Iceland
- C. France
- D. England

7. What are the ingredients of a 'Peach Melba'?

- A. Peaches, yoghurt and lettuce
- B. Peaches, apples and ice cream
- C. Peaches, treacle and yoghurt
- D. Peaches, ice cream and raspberrry puree

8.Who introduced potatoes to Britain?

- A. Sir Richard Attenborough
- B. Emperor Nero
- C. William Blake
- D. Sir Walter Raleigh

9. Which American president was a peanut farmer?

- A. Roosevelt
- B. Kennedy
- C. Reagan
- D. Carter

ANSWERS: 1.(C) 2.(B) 3.(D) 4.(A) 5.(D) 6.(C)
7.(D) 8.(D) 9.(D)

UNCLE $CROOGE
in BUSY DONATOR
THANK YOU FOR YOUR DONATION TO "BE KIND TO ANIMALS," SIR. HERE'S YOUR DONATOR BADGE!
THANKS! I'M ALWAYS GLAD TO GIVE A PENNY TO A WORTHY CAUSE!
D-4214 / KU3590

HOW ABOUT A DONATION FOR "BE KIND TO ANIMALS," MR. McDUCK?
SORRY, BOYS, BUT I ALREADY DONATED A PENNY! SEE MY BADGE?
CLINK
CLINK

WOULD YOU LIKE TO DONATE SOMETHING, SIR?
JINGLE
CLINK
MAIL
GOOD GRIEF!

OOH, I'M SORRY! I DIDN'T SEE THE BADGE ON YOUR COAT! HAVE A NICE DAY!
IF I KEEP GETTING STOPPED BY THESE DONATION NUTS, I'LL NEVER GET BACK TO THE OFFICE!

HA! I'VE GOT AN IDEA!

THANK YOU FOR VOLUNTEERING TO COLLECT DONATIONS FOR US, MR. McDUCK! WE SURE APPRECIATE IT!
"BE KIND TO ANIMALS"

HA! NOW I CAN GET BACK TO THE OFFICE WITHOUT BEING PESTERED AND COLLECT SOME MONEY FOR A GOOD CAUSE AT THE SAME TIME!
JINGLE
CLINK
End

CHIP 'N DALE
RESCUE RANGERS
RIDDLES
THINK HARD
A
B
C
D
E
Monterey
Zipper
Gadget and Dale
Chip and Dale
Dale
GADGET
The Rescue Rangers are all mixed up! Can you unscramble their thoughts and match the right bubble to the right Rescue Ranger?
TEA FOR FIVE
X
Monterey decided to have a party, he sat at the place marked x. Zipper was placed to his left and Dale was to the right of Chip. Gadget was to the left of Chip, so who was seated on the right of Monterey?
F
T
A
C
A
T
Gadget is not just a wizard inventor, she's also an ace at juggling cubes. Can you find the name of the pesky villain hidden in the letters?
Answers:
Think Hard: Zipper wasn't looking where he was going! He flew into a wall, so is seeing stars: Bubble D. Monterey is looking for revenge as someone has stolen his favourite cheese: Bubble A. Gadget is giving Dale a mean look for spilling her coffee: Bubble C. Chip is fuming! Dale has broken his statue: Bubble E. Dale is a vain chipmunk! He has fallenin love with his reflection: Bubble B. Tea for five: Gadget sat to the right of Monterey Juggling: Fat Cat

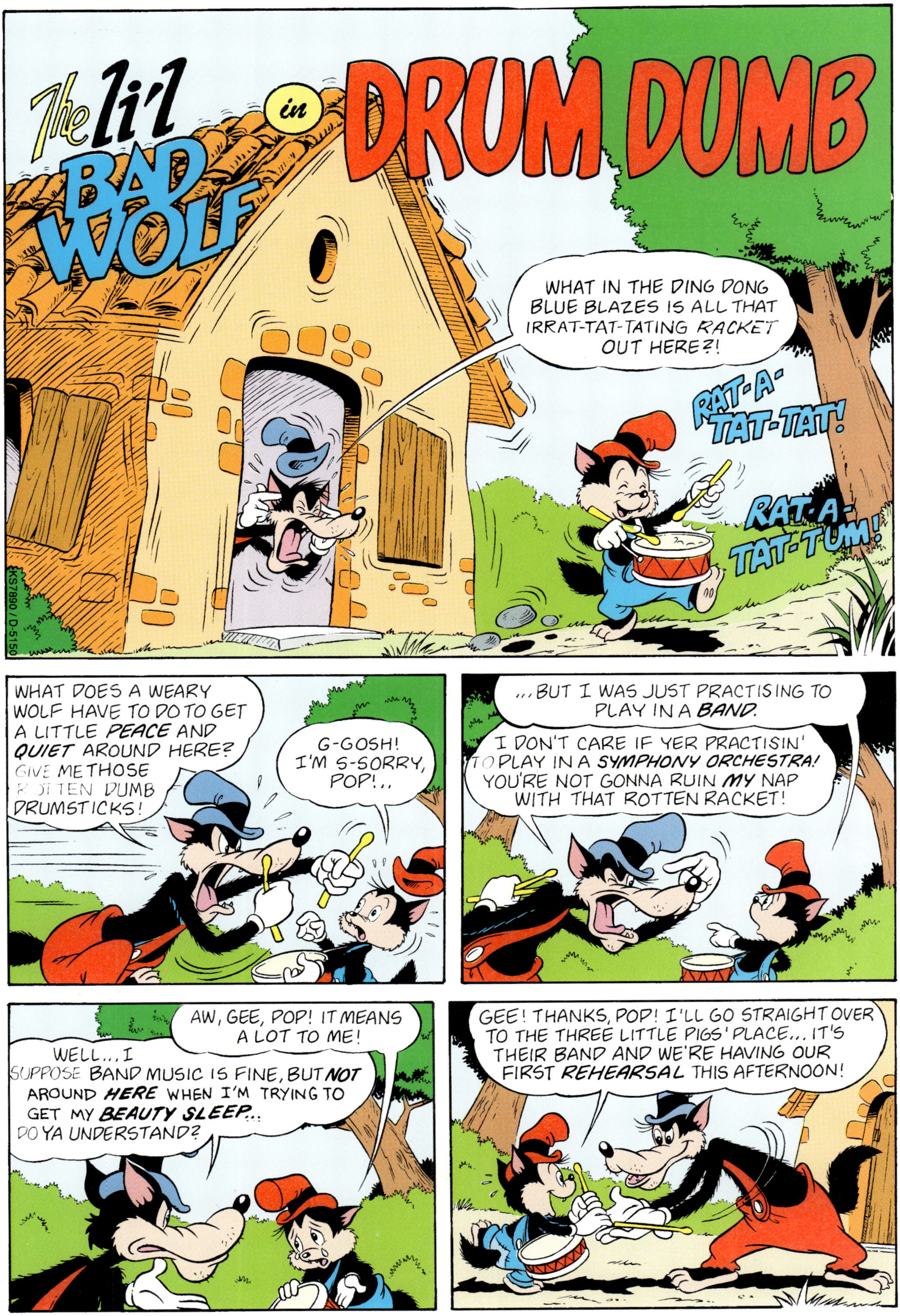

The Li'l Bad Wolf in Drum Dumb

WHAT IN THE DING DONG BLUE BLAZES IS ALL THAT IRRAT-TAT-TATING *RACKET* OUT HERE?!

RAT-A-TAT-TAT!

RAT-A-TAT-TUM!

KS7890 / D-5150

Er... BEFORE YOU GO BACK TO SLEEP I WONDER IF I COULD ASK YOU A REAL BIG FAVOUR POP?
?

THE THREE LITTLE PIGS' UNCLE WART IS COMING OVER FROM HOG HOLLOW AND HE DOESN'T HAVE AN INSTRUMENT TO PLAY...

...AND I WAS WONDERING IF WE COULD BORROW THAT BIG OL' DRUM YOU'VE GOT STOWED AWAY IN THE ATTIC... Hmmm?.. PLEASE?
GRRRR!

WHY SHOULD I LEND SOMETHING TO THE THREE LITTLE PIGS AND THEIR LOWLIFE FAMILY? BAH! I'D RATHER...

...WAIT A MINUTE, ZEKE OL' BOY... ME THINKS YOU HAVE THE BEGINNINGS OF A BRIGHT IDEA!

Er... WHERE DID YOU SAY YOU WERE HOLDING THIS BAND REHEARSAL, SON?
AT THE THREE LITTLE PIGS' HOUSE.

Hmmmmm... ON SECOND THOUGHT, I THINK THIS MUSICAL ENDEAVOUR SHOULD BE AIDED IN EVERY POSSIBLE WAY. OF COURSE, I'LL LEND MY BIG DRUM TO THE THREE LITTLE PIGS!

I'LL GET IT OUT OF THE ATTIC AND LEAVE IT OUTSIDE OUR FRONT DOOR. TELL YOUR PIGGIE FRIENDS THEY CAN PICK IT UP WHEN THEY NEED IT. HEH-HEH!
THANKS, POP!

AS A CONNOISSEUR OF FINE MUSIC IT IS MY DUTY TO SEE THAT THE OLD DRUM IS PUT TO GOOD USE! HEE-HEE-HEE!

AS A GENTLEMAN OF CULTURE I FEEL IT IS MY DUTY TO CONTRIBUTE TO THE ARTS... HUFFFFFF!

I'VE ALWAYS APPRECIATED AN ALL-PIG BAND-- ESPECIALLY ROASTED WITH APPLE SAUCE! HO-HO-HO!

BUT, I'M AFRAID I'LL HAVE TO MAKE A FEW MODIFICATIONS, FIRST!

NOW TO PUT MY MASTER PLAN INTO OPERATION!

ALL I HAVE TO DO IS CUT A HATCH IN THE SIDE OF MY DRUM...
SAW! SAW! SAW!

AND FIX IT BACK IN PLACE-- WITH HINGES!
SCREW SCREW

A MASTERPIECE, IF I MAY SAY SO! HEH-HEH!

Heh! MIGHT AS WELL CLIMB INSIDE RIGHT NOW!

WUFF! IT SURE IS A TIGHT SQUEEZE! ...PANT!...

...BUT NOW I'M ALL READY TO SPRING A TRAP ON THOSE SILLY PIGS AND THEIR HAMMY UNCLE! FOUR PORKERS FOR THE PRICE OF ONE!

BRILLIANT! THAT'S WHAT IT IS! BRILLIANT!

MEANWHILE, AT THE HOUSE OF THE THREE LITTLE PIGS...
TOOT-TOOT!
BLAH-BLAH-BLAH!
SCRAPE-SCRINGE!
RAT-A-TAT-TAT!

IT'S ABOUT TIME YOU THREE WENT AND GOT THAT DRUM FROM THE BIG BAD WOLF... I'LL STAY HERE AND WAIT FOR UNCLE WART.
OKAY, PRACTICAL... C'MON, MEN!

IT'S A GOOD THING WE BROUGHT A WHEELBARROW WITH US.
I DON'T THINK WE'D EVER BE ABLE TO CARRY A GREAT BIG DRUM LIKE THAT.

OOF! IT'S EVEN HEAVIER THAN I THOUGHT IT WOULD BE!

I'M ALWAYS AFRAID THE BIG BAD WOLF WILL TRY TO NAB US WHEN WE'RE AROUND HIS HOUSE!
RELAX, GUYS! MY FATHER IS IN A VERY GENEROUS MOOD-- HE LENT US HIS DRUM, DIDN'T HE?

ANYHOW, THERE'S NO SIGN OF HIM TODAY!
HEE-HEE-HEE!

GET THE DRUM UNLOADED QUICK, FELLAS! UNCLE WART IS HERE AND HE'S READY TO START PLAYING.
GREAT!

LET'S TAKE IT INSIDE-- HE'S WAITING FOR US.

ANY MINUTE NOW I CAN PUT MY PLAN INTO ACTION! I'LL JUMP OUT AND GRAB ALL FOUR PIGGIES!

BASH
!!!
BASH
CRASH

WOW! THIS IS GREAT! I'VE BEEN WANTIN' TO PLAY THE BIG, BASS DRUM EVER SINCE I WAS THE RUNT OF THE LITTER!

LET'S SEE HOW HARD I CAN HIT IT!

BOOOOOOOM!
FLAP

BOOOOOOOM!
WHIZZZZZZZZ
SPLAT

WELL, I'LL BE...
TWEET! TWEET!

...IF IT ISN'T MY OLD PAL, ZEKE WOLF! HOW NICE OF HIM TO DROP IN TO HELP US OUT WITH OUR BAND PRACTISE.

I'VE GOT JUST THE JOB FOR A GREAT MAESTRO LIKE YOU!
MOAN!

GOSH, POP! I DIDN'T KNOW YOU WERE A GREAT MAESTRO!
WHIMPER!

I ALWAYS KNEW ZEKE WAS A PATRON OF THE ARTS!
YEAH, BUT I DIDN'T EXPECT TO GET DRUMMED OUT OF TOWN FOR IT! MOAN!
SCRINGE
BOOM BOOM
BOOM
TOOT TOOT
BLAH BLAH BLAH
RAT-A-TAT
End

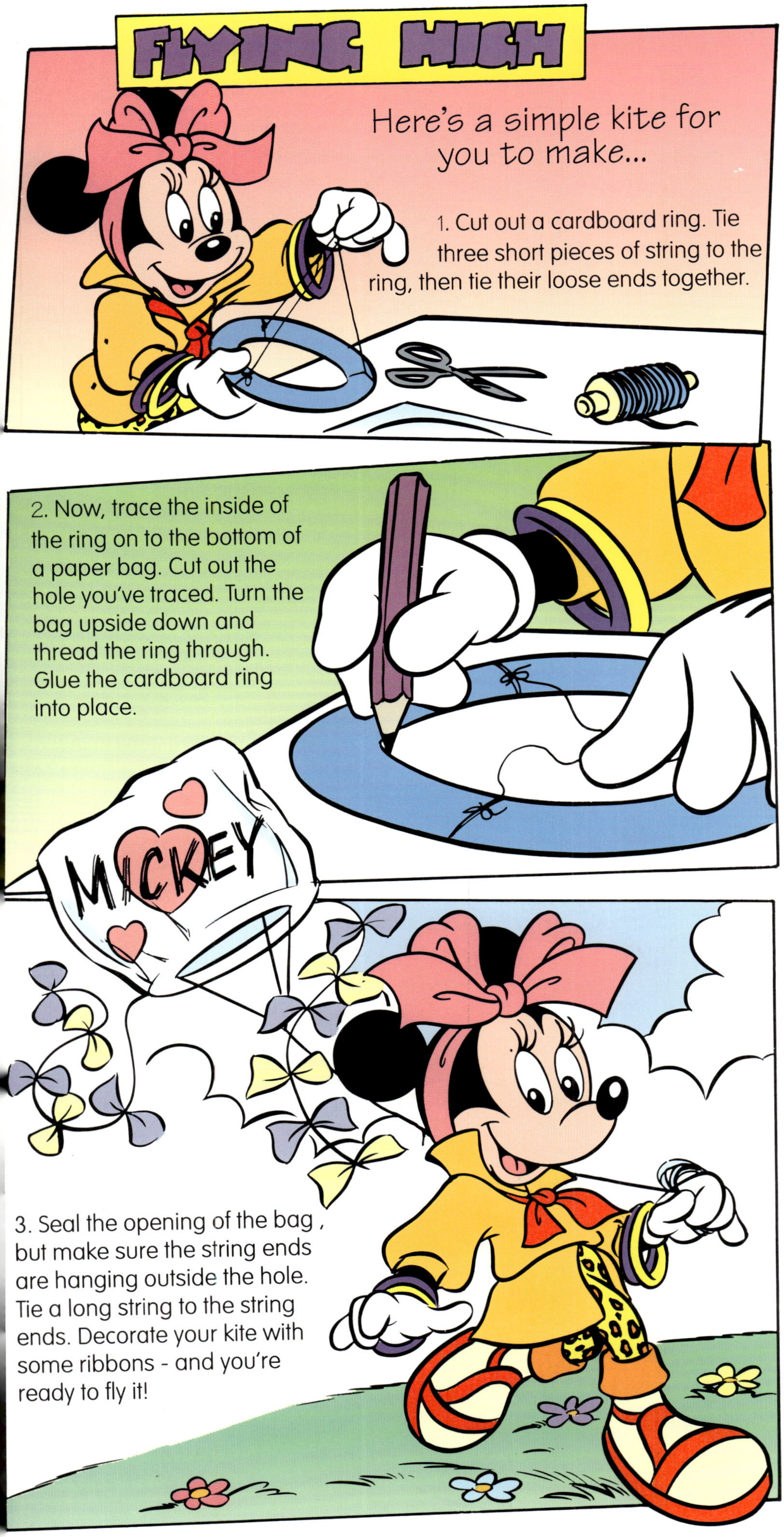

FLYING HIGH

Here's a simple kite for you to make...

1. Cut out a cardboard ring. Tie three short pieces of string to the ring, then tie their loose ends together.

2. Now, trace the inside of the ring on to the bottom of a paper bag. Cut out the hole you've traced. Turn the bag upside down and thread the ring through. Glue the cardboard ring into place.

MICKEY

3. Seal the opening of the bag, but make sure the string ends are hanging outside the hole. Tie a long string to the string ends. Decorate your kite with some ribbons - and you're ready to fly it!

SECRET CODE

Clue: A=1, B=2, and so on.

AMAZING MAZ

This number maze has Louie stumped. In the blank spaces, see if you can write the numbers 1,3,7,8 and 9, so each row adds up to 15 (across, diagonally and downwards)

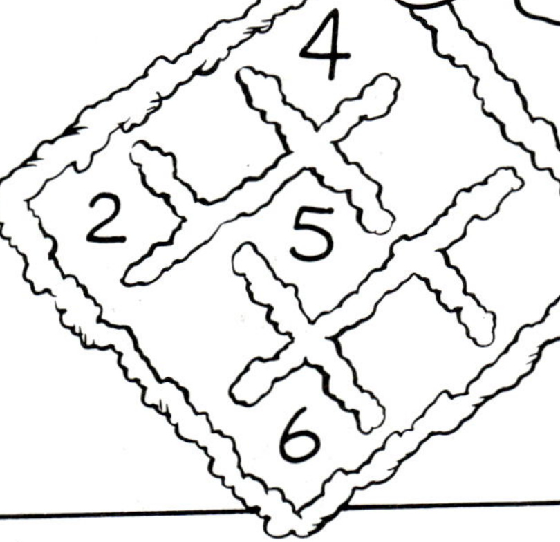

Louie is smart. He can work out the puzzle. Can you?

2 _ | 22 _ 13 _

6 1 _ _

Clue: It's a great animal to use when you want to measure something!

JELLY GALORE

Greedy Huey pigged out on jelly! If you take away all the odd numbers and all the numbers that can be divided by the number 5, you'll find out how many he ate!

Answers:

Secret code: **Q.** What do you call a man with jelly in one ear and custard in the other? **A.** A trifle deaf!

1, 2, 3's: An inchworm!

Jelly galore: Huey ate 6 jellies!